The Stoney Cookbook

ISBN: 978-0-6151-7354-2

Stoney

Cook

Book

Marisa L. Williams

ISBN number: 978-0-6151-7354-2

www.lulu.com/thorisaz

This book is not a book to actually try at home, because drugs are bad. I do not recommend using drugs or in any way harming one's own body. Please do not hold me responsible for anyone who might actually get the bright idea to try some of these things, but if anyone does venture off and attempt a journey, make sure you are as safe and secure as possible.

Thanks to all my friends and family who have helped me along the way. Suggestions were greatly appreciated. To all those silent chefs who helped me compile these ideas, thank you.

Remember, it's not nice to dose an unsuspecting person, such as a parent, authority figure or child. Think before you follow through. Have a nice trip } :)~

Cheers to all!

Marisa

Chocolate Strawberry Mushroom Smoothie

A quarter of mushrooms
A cup of vanilla yogurt
One banana
3 tablespoons chocolate syrup
Pint fresh strawberries

Blend until smooth and serve to four people.

Chocolate Hemp Shake

3 scoops chocolate ice cream
½ cup of milk
3 tablespoons chocolate syrup
An eighth of marijuana, de-seeded and de-stemmed, finely ground

Fill blender with ice, blend until smooth and serve, 4 people.

Hash/Hemp/Mushroom Tea

Boil a quarter of mushrooms (or marijuana, de-seeded) in two cups of water. Strain out solid particles, which can be saved for use in other cooking ventures, if desired. For flavor, add a tablespoon or two of honey and a few squirts of fresh lemon. Serve half-cup portions to four people.

Hash/Hemp/Mushroom Butter

In a pot, melt down a pound of butter, mixing in a quarter of either mushrooms or deseeded marijuana, simmer for five to ten minutes, and strain out solid parts. The leftover particles can be used in other culinary activities. Allow butter to solidify; use as normal or try smothering some mussels.

Psychedelic Pizza

Prepare a pizza as normal, or order a pizza from a restaurant. Decorate with an eighth of mushrooms and sprinkle with ground up, de-stemmed and deseeded marijuana, few pinches. Cover with shredded cheese and bake in oven at 400 degrees for five minutes, until cheese is melted; cheese is optional item.

Cheesy Psychedelic Spinach and Artichoke Dip

Mix a small can of artichoke hearts, drained and cut up if needed, with an 8 oz package of frozen spinach, de-thawed, an 8 oz package of cream cheese, 4 oz of pepperjack cheese, cubed, 4 oz of crumbled feta cheese, diced onion, diced garlic, diced jalapeno pepper, an eighth of mushrooms, a few sprinkles of Italian seasoning, marijuana and Cajun seasoning. A pound of cooked sausage or some bacon bits can be added for meat lovers, or for a seafood twist, try adding either crab or shrimp, cooked separately; seafood should be added in just before serving, so as not to overcook. In a casserole dish, bake the concoction at 350 degrees for about 45 minutes. Allow the mix to cool a bit before serving, so as not to burn your tongue. You can also allow chill the mix and serve it cold with nacho chips if desired. This mix is great to slap on top of sliced

French Bread. Bagel chips are also great to dip
into this mix.

Minty Hemp Brownies

Prepare any brownie mix according to package,
using either hash butter instead of the required oil
or mixing in an eighth of de-stemmed, deseeded
and finely ground marijuana. Take three regular
size or seven mini-sized York Peppermint Patties,
breaking them up into pieces and chunks. Mix
this into the brownie mix and bake as usual, chill
and serve.

Tropical Hemp Brownies

Take any normal brownie recipe, preparing it
with hash butter instead of the required oil (or use
normal oil and simply mix in an eighth of finely
ground, de-stemmed and deseeded marijuana).
Mix in a cup of coconut, a half cup of crushed
macadamia nuts and a cup of white chocolate
chips. Bake according to directions, chill and
serve.

Pizza Surprise

Take a cup of rhubarb, add in either pumpkin, squash or zucchini, keep adding water so it spins smooth in a blender. In your bread machine, instead of water, use the puree, saving the excess for later use. Go about your usual recipe, using organic flour. Once bread is done, slice about an inch thick and top with mozzarella, parmesan, onions, green peppers, and any other cooking herbs, three to seven shakes of ground marijuana. Zap in microwave for a minute until cheese melts, or put in oven at 400 degrees for about ten minutes.

Psychedelic Hot Dogs

In a cup of water, boil a quarter of mushrooms, straining out the solid parts to use as hot dog topping later. Take a marinade injector full of the liquid, poke each hot dog and insert psychedelic liquid. Save excess liquid to add to sauerkraut. If injector method is too complex, boil your hot dogs in a small pan with a quarter of mushrooms until hot dogs split, as a sign they're done, saving both the liquid and solid mushroom parts for later use. Or if chili dogs are preferred, mix in an eighth of finely ground marijuana into chili mix, then top your hot dog wrapped in fresh marijuana leaves at the next family gathering. You ca also top with onions, crushed up nachos, cheese and baked beans or sausage gravy, which can also have mushrooms or marijuana added to it.

Twisty Time Cocoa

In a mug, combine five tablespoons of powdered milk in 8oz of water (mushroom tea water can also be used for an added adventure), a dash of sea salt and three dashes of finely ground marijuana, heat up in microwave for a minute and twenty second, add a small drop of vanilla, a spoonful of cocoa and a squirt of maple syrup. Mix and enjoy.

Trails Mixin' Brownies

Prepare a brownie mix using mushroom butter instead of oil, mixing in an eighth of finely ground deseeded and de-stemmed marijuana, a half cup of crushed peanuts, a cup of candy coated chocolates (M & M's) and a half cup of raisins. Bake as usual, cook and enjoy.

Baked Chicken

In a casserole dish, combine a pound of boneless and skinless chicken cut into chunks, a diced Granny Smith apple, a few chunks of bacon, onion ringlets, one small diced radish, a diced garlic clove, three finely chopped celery stalks, an eighth of ground up and deseeded marijuana, a handful of fresh spinach, Cajun seasoning and two tablespoons of BBQ sauce. Bake at 350 degrees for 45 minutes, until chicken is fully cooked. Serve.

High On Salad

For the salad base, use fresh spinach and marijuana leaves. Top with diced up psychedelic mushrooms, crumbled hard boiled egg, turkey chunks, small ham cubes, bacon bits, blue cheese crumbles, feta cheese crumbles, shredded pepperjack cheese, garbanzo beans, alfalfa sprouts, bean sprouts, shredded carrots, sliced cucumbers, crushed peanuts, pine nuts, almond slivers, diced tomatoes or any other choice of toppings. Instead of dressing, you can sprinkle your salad with fresh lemon, lime or orange juice, top with Italian seasoning, ground up garlic and red pepper, and a few dashes of ground marijuana.

Fruity Styled Salad

Using fresh spinach and marijuana leaves, toss a salad with dried or fresh and deseeded cherries, strawberry chunks, blue berries, black berries, banana chunks, mandarin orange slices, almond slivers, pine nuts, slivered ham chunks, melon chunks, raisins, dried cranberries and fresh grapes. Instead of using a traditional salad dressing, whipped cream can be used, though it may not be the best with ham (an acquired taste). Mix in sprinkles of ground marijuana or chunks of psychedelic mushrooms for an added splendor. You can also layer dishes and include such fruit as apples, pears, peaches, etc.

Baked Ziti Nights

In a large saucepan, cook a pound of ground sausage with a diced onion, diced green pepper, diced garlic, a handful of fresh spinach and a quarter of psychedelic mushrooms. While the sausage is cooking, prepare a pot of boiling water with a dash of salt and a drop of olive oil to cook a box of ziti according to package; penne or other pasta types can also be used. Going back to the sausage, once the meat is cooked, add in a large can of diced or stewed tomatoes with basil and oregano. Sprinkle with Italian seasoning, marjoram and marijuana. Artichoke hearts or peas are optional additions to the pasta creation, as is a splash of white wine into the sauce. Simmer the sauce while the pasta cooks, and just before combining the two, while both piping hot, cut up an 8 oz chunk of mozzarella cheese into tiny cubes to melt within the pasta. Top with parmesan cheese and serve.

Zone-out Lasagna

In a skillet, cook a pound of sausage with diced garlic, green pepper, onion and psychedelic mushrooms. Boil lasagna noodles according to package in a large pot with a small drop of olive oil and a small dash of salt. While that is taking place, in a bowl, combine two eggs, 4 to 6 oz of ricotta cheese, 4 to 6 oz of cottage cheese, 4 oz of feta cheese, 4 oz of shredded mozzarella cheese, a few shakes of black pepper, a small shake of red pepper, an eighth of ground up and deseeded marijuana, a dash of marjoram and a few dashes Italian seasoning. In a large baking dish, layer noodles, Classico or Bertolli's Vodka Sauce, cheese mixture and meat mixture. A layer of spinach or fresh marijuana leaves is optional. Continue layering until all ingredients are exhausted, then sprinkle the top generously with parmesan cheese and shredded mozzarella cheese. Cover with aluminum foil and bake at 325 degrees for an hour, then remove the foil and continue to cook until top cheese layer begins to bubble, slightly browning around edges. Let sit for 20 minutes before serving; excellent the next day.

Garlic Bread Daze

Slice a loaf of French bread lengthwise and flip upwards. Use mushroom or hash butter to butter bread; if hard to spread, cut into slivers, spread out periodically to melt evenly into the bread. Dust with garlic powder, ground up marijuana and Italian seasoning. Top with psychedelic mushrooms, fresh tomato slices and slabs of mozzarella; spinach or fresh marijuana leaves optional. Bake at 400 for ten minutes, until cheese is melted and slightly browned. Serve with your favorite pasta dishes or add turkey, ham and bacon for an awesome club sandwich.

Chicken Pot Pie

Form a nine-inch pie crust to a pie tin; either prepare your own crust or buy frozen, but two crusts are needed. In a pot, combine chunks of boneless and skinless chicken with diced garlic, green pepper, onion, carrots and psychedelic mushrooms. Use a dab of hash butter to ensure the chicken does not stick. Just as the chicken is done cooking, add in three tablespoons of cream cheese, mix thoroughly, a small can of peas, a small can of corn, crumbled feta cheese, shredded taco cheese, a dash of Italian seasoning, a dash of Cajun seasoning, a dash of marjoram, a dash of marijuana, and a dash of black pepper. Pour into pie tin and cover with other crust. Bake at 450 for 15 minutes, until crust is golden, or bake according to the package of the crust. After pulling it out of the oven, melt some hash butter onto the top crust of the pie. Allow to cool before serving.

Afraid 'O Chicken?

In a skillet, cook a pound of chunked boneless, skinless chicken with diced garlic, red pepper, green pepper, onion, broccoli and psychedelic mushrooms. Add a dash of Italian seasoning, a dash of marjoram and a dash of ground marijuana. Boil a package of penne pasta. Combine chicken with pasta, Alfredo sauce and marijuana.

Special Salsa

In as small of pieces as possible, dice up garlic, onion, green pepper, red pepper, jalapeno pepper, tomato, psychedelic mushrooms, cilantro, parsley, shallots, a small radish and a mango. Squirt a small amount of lemon and lime to preserve veggies. Add pinches of Italian seasoning and ground marijuana.

Fruit Zone Salsa

As tiny as you can, dice up an onion, yellow pepper, jalapeno pepper, red pepper, a peach, pineapple, cilantro, parsley, a pear, psychedelic mushrooms. Dash with fresh orange and lime juices to preserve, and add dashes of Italian seasoning and ground marijuana. Serve with nacho chips.

Nacho Average Layer

In a skillet, cook a pound of ground meat with diced onions, green peppers, garlic, and psychedelic mushrooms. Add a packet of nacho seasoning and a few dashes of finely ground and deseeded marijuana. Just before the meat is taken off the heat, add in a can of refried beans and a few more pinches of pot. In a dish, layer Doritos, freshly sliced marijuana leaves and spinach, meat/beans, shredded nacho cheese, olives, salsa, sour cream. Guacamole is optional.

Sinful Salmon

In a skillet, melt three tablespoons of hash butter with two tablespoons of cream cheese, diced garlic, psychedelic mushrooms and yellow pepper; mix in a few dashes of Old Bay seasoning and freshly ground marijuana. Cook a salmon filet in this, and just before the fish is done cooking, add a small can of peas. Sprinkle with parsley and marijuana before devouring.

Veggie Stir Shocker

In a skillet, melt a generous dab of hash butter with fresh garlic, diced onion, green pepper, red pepper, broccoli, asparagus, psychedelic mushrooms and yellow squash. Serve on top of fresh spinach and marijuana leaves with shredded carrots and bean sprouts for crunch. Sprinkle with Italian seasoning and ground marijuana.

A Toasty Roast

Put a roast in a slow cooker, along with diced carrots, onion, green pepper, garlic, psychedelic mushrooms, potatoes, an eighth of deseeded and de-stemmed marijuana, Cajun seasoning and a beef bouillon cube. Slow cook until meat is falling apart tender. Add more just a titch more Cajun and marijuana before serving.

Scrambled Egg Zone

In a bowl, mix a half dozen eggs with a splash of milk, crumbled feta cheese, dash of black pepper, dash of Cajun season, dash of Italian season, dash of ground marijuana, dash of marjoram, diced green pepper, red pepper, onion, garlic and psychedelic mushrooms. Additional add-in suggestions are crab, shrimp, lobster, turkey, deviled ham, bacon bits, broccoli and/or asparagus. Pour into a skillet pre-heated to medium with a generous dab of hash butter melted in it. Stir constantly until egg is cooked, being careful not to scorch the bottom or overcook.

Psychedelic Shooters

Boil a quarter of mushrooms into a cup of water, filtering out the solid parts and saving them for later usage in other cooking ventures, such as throwing the solid pieces onto a pizza. On the side, add ice cubes to a half cup of vanilla vodka, making an ice cold cup of iced vanilla vodka. Dissolve your favorite flavor of jello into the boiling water; strawberry, orange and lime flavors work especially well with vanilla vodka. In a dish, combine the cup of hot mushroom water with the cup of cold vanilla vodka water, then pour into individual shooter cups, plastic Dixie cups, or pour into a dish and cut into fun sized jiggler shapes after cooling at least an hour.

Fluffy Munchies

Prepare a package of chocolate pudding, mixing in three tablespoons of crunchy peanut butter and a few generous dashes of ground marijuana. Cool until set. In individual serving bowls, break up angel food cake into tiny chunks, then top with chocolate peanut butter pudding. Layer cut up banana, marshmallow, whipped cream with a few dashes of marijuana mixed in. Top with chopped nuts, nutmeg, chocolate syrup, more marijuana sprinkles, fresh strawberries or blueberries, hot fudge, melted peanut butter, peanut butter cup chunks, chocolate sprinkles, your favorite ice cream and/or some cherries.

Stonily Stacked Waffles

Combine an eighth of ground up marijuana and psychedelic mushrooms into a few cups of your favorite flavor of ice cream, slightly melting to make the mixing easier, then stick it back in your freezer until later. The bottom layer is a chocolate chip waffle, covered in hard shell chocolate syrup, like one would used on an old-fashioned ice cream cone. Top with your marijuana ice cream, whipped cream, fresh berries, sprinkles, chocolate chips, shredded coconut, crushed nuts, candy coated chocolates, crushed cookies, brownie chunks, cinnamon roll pieces, chocolate syrup, gummy bears, candy bar chunks, more finely ground mushrooms and marijuana, hot fudge, marshmallow, banana, melted peanut butter, butterscotch or your favorite toppings and a cherry.

7 Layer Haze

Cut a half cup of hash or mushroom butter into chunks, and melt it in the bottom of a pan by sticking it in the oven at 350 degrees for a moment. Crush up two cups of chocolate graham crackers, mixing the crackers with the hash butter and pressing it into the bottom of the pan carefully. Sprinkle with a cup and a half of chocolate chips and a cup and a half of peanut butter chips (butterscotch can be used instead). Crush a cup of walnuts and sprinkle onto the mix, along with a few sprinkles of either finely ground marijuana or mushrooms. Pour a 14 oz can of sweetened condensed milk over the layers. Cover with a cup of coconut flakes. Bake about 27 minutes, until edges are browned, then cool and cut into bars; serve and enjoy.

Hash Kissed Brownies

Grease a 13 x 9 baking pan and preheat oven to 350 degrees. Combine 2/3 cup cocoa, a half teaspoon of baking soda, and 1/3 cup of melted hash butter. Bring a half cup of water and an eighth of mushrooms to boil, then strain out the solid parts. Add the mushroom water to the hash butter mix. Stir in two cups of sugar, two eggs, a teaspoon of vanilla and another 1/3 cup of hash butter. Blend in a cup and a half of unbleached flour and a quarter teaspoon of sea salt. Stir in two cups of a combination of chocolate chips, peanut butter chips, Hershey Kisses, Reese's chunks. You can also add in up to a cup of finely chopped nuts, too. Spread batter in pan and bake for 35 to 40 minutes, until edges begin to retract from the sides of the pan. Cool completely before cutting and serving, unless you want to serve it warm with a scoop of ice cream melting down the edges. If so, feel free to garnish as a sundae with whipped cream, ground peanuts, chocolate sauce and a cherry.

Peanut Hash Blossoms

Preheat oven to 375 degrees. Beat together a half cup of hash butter and ¾ cup of creamy peanut butter. Beat in 1/3 cup of sugar and 1/3 cup of brown sugar, followed by an egg, two tablespoons of milk and a teaspoon of vanilla. Combine a cup and a half of unbleached flour, a teaspoon of baking soda and a half teaspoon of sea salt, slowly adding it to the mix. Shape dough into balls about an inch around. Roll in large grain sugar, such as the natural Hawaiian styled sugar chunks. Place on cookie sheet and bake about 8 minutes or until lightly browned. As soon as you take them out of the oven, place three peanut butter filled Hershey kisses on top of each cookie, pressing the kisses down into the dough. Cool and serve.

Macadamia Nut Buzzer

Bring six tablespoons of hash butter and a third cup of mushroom butter to room temperature. Preheat oven to 350 degrees. Beat the butters, adding a half cup of brown sugar and a third cup of granulated sugar. Add an egg and a teaspoon and a half of vanilla. Stir together a cup and a third of unbleached flour, a half teaspoon of baking soda, a few sprinkles of finely ground marijuana, a few sprinkles of finely ground psychedelic mushrooms and a half teaspoon of sea salt; gradually add this to the mixture. Stir in a cup of white chocolate chunks (chocolate chips can be used instead) and a half cup of crushed macadamia nuts. For an added treat, add a half cup of coconut. Drop teaspoonfuls of the dough onto an ungreased cookie sheet. Bake about ten minutes or until edges are slightly browned. Cool, serve and enjoy.

Stoney Road Brownies

Heat oven to 450 degrees and generously grease a 9-inch square pan with hemp butter. Melt a half cup of hash or mushroom butter and 3 oz of unsweetened chocolate over low heat in a medium saucepan. Stir frequently to ensure the bottom does not scorch. In a small bowl, combine a cup of unbleached flour, ¾ teaspoon of baking powder, a half teaspoon of sea salt, a few sprinkles of finely ground marijuana and a few generous sprinkles of finely ground psychedelic mushrooms. In a large bowl, beat three eggs with a cup and a half of granulated sugar and a teaspoon and a half of vanilla. Beat mixture until thick. Gradually combine the egg mix with the chocolate mix, then stir in the flour mix. Spread evenly in the pan and bake for 25 to 30 minutes, until edges begin to pull away from the sides of the pan. Remove from oven. Sprinkle with a half cup of chopped peanuts, a half cup of chocolate chips, a half cup of mini marshmallows and a quarter cup of warmed chocolate fudge topping that has a few more sprinkles of marijuana and mushrooms blended in it. Continue to bake 8 to 11 minutes or until lightly browned, then cool, cut and serve. Excellent to serve with a scoop of ice cream while still warm, causing the ice cream to melt in with brownie.

Peanut Fudge Daze

Mix a half cup of milk in a saucepan with a pound of confectioner's sugar. Let boil for four minutes, slowly adding an eighth of finely ground marijuana or psychedelic mushrooms, then take off of heat. Add 13 oz of peanut butter and a 7 oz jar of marshmallow cream. Put in an 8x8 pan greased down with hash butter. Cool before serving.

Hazy Chocolate Icing

Bring a quarter pound of either hash or mushroom butter to room temperature. In a large mixing bowl, mix the hash butter with a pound of confectioner's sugar, three tablespoons of cocoa, a teaspoon of vanilla, and four and a half tablespoons of milk. Beat at medium speed until well blended. For an added kick, blend in a few dash of finely ground marijuana or psychedelic mushrooms with a cup of chocolate chips.

French Banana Toasted

In a bowl, mash a ripe banana, stirring in two teaspoons of frozen orange juice concentrate and a few generous sprinkles of finely ground marijuana. With four pieces of cinnamon raisin bread, spread the banana mix on two slices, placing the other two slices on top, so it forms two sandwiches. In a pie tin, whisk two large egg whites with a quarter cup of milk and another sprinkle of ground marijuana. Soak the sides of the bread in this egg mix. Mix a quarter cup of plain or strawberry yogurt with a sprinkle of ground marijuana, and set aside. Melt a teaspoon of hash butter in a skillet over low heat. Cook the sandwiches over medium-low heat for about 5 minutes, until edges brown, then add another teaspoon of hash butter to the pan before cooking the other sides of the sandwiches. Serve topped with the enhanced yogurt and garnish with freshly cut strawberries or slices of banana, if desired.

Banana Hash Bread

Preheat oven to 350 degrees and grease a large loaf pan with hash butter. Mix three cups unbleached flour, 2/3 cup of brown sugar, 2/3 cup natural cane sugar, a teaspoon of baking soda, a teaspoon of baking powder, a teaspoon of cinnamon and a pinch of sea salt. Mash three large bananas, usually bananas that are just starting to turn brown are the easiest to work with and have some of the best flavor; if thinking of baking ahead of time, buy bananas, and when they are just turning, put them in the freezer, pulling them out to thaw early in the day you decide to bake. Combine a couple eggs with a third cup of vanilla soy milk, a couple tablespoons of applesauce, a teaspoon and a half of vanilla and an eighth of marijuana, ground, deseeded and de-stemmed. Mix all ingredients with a half cup of chopped walnuts (optional), a half cup of cranberries or golden raisins, or a third cup of dried banana slices. You can also add in cut-up caramel squares for an extra gooey experience, or add in chopped peanuts. Bake in prepared loaf pan for an hour and twenty minutes, until a fork in the center comes out clean. While warm, coat the top with a few pats of hash butter. Serve with caramel sauce or additional hash butter.

Soy Stoned Shake

Fill a blender with ice, a few generous pinches of ground marijuana, a heaping spoonful or two of peanut butter, a banana and chocolate soy milk. Blend and serve. For an even creamier blend, cut back on some of the ice and blend in a scoop of soy ice cream.

Carmel Apple Dazer

Preheat oven to 350 degrees and grease a large loaf pan with hash butter. Mix three cups unbleached flour, 2/3 cup of brown sugar, 2/3 cup natural cane sugar, a teaspoon of baking soda, a teaspoon of baking powder, a teaspoon of cinnamon and a pinch of sea salt. Combine a couple eggs with a third cup of vanilla soy milk, a couple tablespoons of applesauce, a half cup of diced Granny Smith apples (either one large or two small apples), half cup of cut up caramel cubes, one half cup of chocolate coated raisins, a teaspoon and a half of vanilla and an eighth of marijuana, ground, deseeded and de-stemmed. Mix all ingredients with any desired optional item, such as half cup of chopped walnuts or a third cup of dried banana slices. Bake in prepared loaf pan for an hour and twenty minutes, until a fork in the center comes out clean. While warm, coat the top with a few pats of hash butter. Serve with caramel sauce or additional hash butter.

Enhanced Angel Cake

Prepare a package of pudding with half the required milk, so it gets extra thick, mixing in an eighth of finely ground and deseeded marijuana. Mix this with a half tub of whipped cream and a small can of mandarin orange slices. Cut a prepared angel food cake in half, coating the two layers with the whipped frosting, placing the layers back into position. Sprinkle generously with flaked coconut and serve.

Twisty Zucchini Tart

In a medium bowl, combine a cup and a half of unbleached flour with a quarter teaspoon of sea salt. Cut in a half cup of hash butter until it is the size of small peas. Sprinkle a quarter cup of cold water over dough until it begins to hold shape when pushed together. Cover and chill for at least an hour. Roll out the dough until it is two inches larger than the pie tin. Fit the dough into the pan. Preheat oven to 350 degrees. Prick the dough with a fork several times and bake in oven until golden. Mix two tablespoons of melted hash butter with a few dashes of basil, a dash of sea salt, a dash of black pepper and a finely diced garlic clove. Cover the bottom of the pie with a quarter cup of gruyere cheese, then cover the cheese with ten whole basil leaves. Chop a quarter of psychedelic mushrooms, a small zucchini and a large tomato, layering on top of the cheese, and sprinkle generously with the hash butter mixture. Extra cheese can be added as a topping if desired, such as feta or shredded parmesan. Bake about ten minutes and serve warm.

Creamed Veggie Dip

Mix an 8 oz package of cream cheese with 6 oz of sour cream. Blend in a package of dry ranch dressing mix (dry onion soup mix works, too) and a few generous sprinkles of ground marijuana. Finely dice celery, an onion, a green pepper, a few psychedelic mushrooms and a tomato to add into the blend. Serve with crackers, nachos or carrot sticks.

Blueberry Salsa Slam

In a food processor (or finely chop), combine the following: a pint of fresh and de-stemmed blueberries, green onions, a Vidalia onion, a sweet pepper, a couple celery stalks, a few cilantro sprigs, a dash of lime juice, a dash of lemon juice, one half banana, a Granny Smith apple, an eighth of de-stemmed and deseeded finely ground marijuana or psychedelic mushrooms (or a combination of the two), a jalapeno pepper, a garlic clove, a dash of Italian seasoning, a dash of black pepper or even a very tiny dash of red pepper flakes if extremely hot is desired, and one small radish. Serve with blue corn chips.

Corn Fused Dip

Combine a can of sweet corn with finely diced green and red peppers, a garlic clove, a red onion, a few cilantro sprigs, a large tomato, a few psychedelic mushrooms, a dash of lime juice, a dash of lemon juice, a dash of black pepper, a dash of Cajun season, a dash of Italian season and a few dashes of finely ground marijuana. Mix well and dip with your favorite corn chips, nachos or serve as a relish with Mexican styled food.

Blackout Bean Dip

Prepare a cup of brown rice, boiling a couple diced psychedelic mushrooms, a large diced tomato and an onion in with two cups of water until it is all absorbed by the rice; stir constantly towards the end to ensure the rice does not burn at the bottom of the pot. Meanwhile, prepare a pound of ground meat with some diced onion, green pepper, a diced garlic clove, taco seasoning, a few generous sprinkles of ground marijuana and a couple diced psychedelic mushrooms. Mix a can of refried beans with an eighth of finely ground, de-stemmed and deseeded marijuana. Chop up a red pepper, some green onion, a few psychedelic mushrooms and a garlic clove. Mix with beans; warming the mix in the microwave for about 30 seconds will make it easier to stir. In a 13 x 9 dish, layer the rice, then the beans, followed by the meat. Top with sour cream, salsa and guacamole, then serve with Doritos.

Fire Chicken Wraps

Cut up a pound of boneless, skinless chicken breast into bit-size chunks, then cook it in a pan with green pepper, red pepper, jalapeno pepper, onion, garlic clove and a few psychedelic mushrooms. Add a packet of fajita mix and a few generous sprinkles of ground marijuana. Roll into a wrap with radish slivers, fresh spinach, shredded taco cheese, salsa, sour cream, refried beans or Spanish rice. Sprinkle one more small dash of ground marijuana and black pepper on each serving. If using burrito shells, dampen a paper towel, set up to three shells on a plate, cover with the dampened paper towel and zap in the microwave for up to 20 seconds, usually about ten seconds each. This will allow for easier rolling.

Stoned White Chili

In a large pot, cook a pound of boneless and skinless chicken breast cup up into bit-sized chunks. Add diced onion, green pepper, red pepper, jalapeno pepper, garlic clove, celery stalks and a couple-few psychedelic mushrooms. Continue to add a can of green beans, a can of sweet corn, two large cans of great northern beans, two cans of chicken broth, a few generous dashes of ground marijuana, a chicken bouillon cube, dash sea salt, few dashes ground black pepper, one small dash ground red pepper, dash of Cajun seasoning, dash of chicken seasoning, dash of marjoram, dash of Italian seasoning and a dash of turmeric. Simmer down and for bean variation, try a can of black beans with a can of great northern beans. If desired, add a dash or two of your favorite hot sauce.

I'm Fried Rice

In one large pot, simmer two cups of brown rice with four cups of water. As this cooks, slowly add in diced onion, diced tomato, diced psychedelic mushrooms and a small pat of hash butter with a dash of sea salt. In another pot, cook a half dozen strips of bacon, previously cut into chunks (in a pinch, I've even used salad bacon bits, adding it a little later), with a half pound of diced ham. Sometimes, it's easier to use the previously cooked small ham cubes that's at the store. A pound of sausage can also be substituted, or a pound of meat combining the ham, sausage and bacon bits, even a pound of chicken if seeking to cook healthier. Basically, you need a pound of meat, your choice, though I would not use hamburger. You can substitute a pound of crawfish though. Either way, this is going to be cooked with green pepper, onion, jalapeno pepper, celery stalks, garlic clove, psychedelic mushrooms, a few generous dashes of ground marijuana, a few dashes Cajun seasoning, dash Italian seasoning, a dash of hot sauce, a dash of marjoram, small dash of dill and a sprinkle of celery seed. Asparagus, broccoli and spinach are optional add-ins for vegetarian substitutions or just for extra greens intake. If you like it hotter, add a dash of red pepper. As the meat is done cooking, add a can of diced tomatoes with chili peppers (you can split this up between the rice and the meat mix if desired), along with two cans of black beans. Stir this mix to make sure the bottom does not scorch. If timed right, this should be done about the same time as the rice. Serve a scoop of each on a dish. Garnish with fresh parsley or cilantro and a sprinkling of shredded cheese, if desired. A tiny dollop of sour cream may also be desired by some.

High-On Café

Fill a blender with an eighth of either marijuana (deseeded and de-stemmed) OR psychedelic mushrooms, three to five scoops of coffee flavored ice cream (other flavors work just as well, especially chocolate chip cookie dough), three shots of coffee flavored liquor, three shots of coffee and a few cubes of ice. Blend and served garnished with chocolate sauce, whipped cream and two cherries sticking out of the top of the straw (slide one stem in halfway, then the other, shoving the stems down the straw so just the cherries pop out the top). You can also put a couple chocolate covered coffee beans into the whipped cream.

Mint Mind Melter

In a blender, mix an eighth of cleaned psychedelic mushrooms with a few pinches of ground and deseeded marijuana and three to five scoops of mint chocolate chip ice cream. Add a shot of crème de menthe, Van Gogh chocolate flavored vodka, Bailey's, and a shot of Godiva chocolate liquor. Blend with ice and slurp down.

Crazy Cookie Crumbler

In a blender, combine one sixteenth of an ounce of psychedelic mushrooms with one sixteenth of an ounce of ground and deseeded marijuana, a few scoops of cookie dough or Oreo cookie ice cream, one shot chocolate vodka, one shot vanilla vodka, a shot of Bailey's, a splash of milk or cream and some ice cubes. Blend, serve and enjoy.

Krazy Kamikaze

Since a kamikaze is my favorite drink, and I usually only drink it one way, made with vanilla vodka, I will share within this recipe a little bit more than I will in the rest of the book. Here seems like a good place to spell out the dilemma I have faced with this book. Do I stick with just weed and mushrooms, because they're natural, more legal and more accepted than some of the other things out there? Or do I say fuck it and just throw out a cookbook full of all kinds of drugs. Then I got to thinking about the different kinds of drugs there are, and how I would cook with them. Most of the things I could think of came in powdered form, such as cocaine, heroin, meth, molly, E, and whatever else. For those things, you don't need very much, so cooking can become quite dangerous for people who just get excited and dump enough to overdose a small village. For this reason, I decided to stay away from it. In reality, I don't really promote those harder drugs anyways, but I do realize that there are people out there who do them, and I'm not saying I've never tried any of them, as I'm a sinner like everyone else. What I mentioned in my first cook book, Marisa's Ultimate Party Guide - which is an actual cookbook with drinks, appetizers, main courses and all kinds of stuff, including many pirated and slightly changed to avoid copyright hassle recipes from gourmet places around the world – is that sometimes eating drugs may be better than say sticking a needle in your arm. Sure, I knew that coca-cola was named such because when it first came out, it contained a small amount of cocaine, so I knew people have obviously ingested the same drugs that they stick in a needle, just in different formats. Really, the idea of cooking with cocaine I must credit to my former neighbor Charlie, a flamboyant gay man who had a bit of a cocaine habit. His solution to weening himself off when he got too out of control was simply to cook with it in his food, as opposed to snorting a rail up his nose or grabbing a needle. What works easiest, he suggests, is dissolving any sort of powder into a liquid form. Thus, drinks become the obvious choice. Instead of giving The Bartender's Bible with a shot of your choice of powder, I'll suggest that you simply pick your favorite drink and dissolve whatever into that. Now, please be careful; remember in the digestive track that less is more. You don't want to tear your stomach apart in the process; so literally, you only need about half a teaspoon. Remember, you can always get seconds, but most importantly, since the drug does not go directly into your lungs as it would in smoking or directly into your bloodstream as it would in using a needle, eating drugs can take a little more time for effect. Anticipate waiting about an hour and a half to feel it start to kick in. That means, don't just do a shot of something, then thinks it's not working and do another, as you haven't given it time to kick in. Believe me, just about the time you want to start cursing me and saying I'm full of shit, you'll be laid back. Anyhow, enough of a lecture; I think you get the point. For a kamikaze the way I like, pour vanilla vodka, Rosie's sweet lime and Triple Sec at about equal parts...maybe a little more vodka and a little less lime depending. Dissolve a small pinch of your choice of powder into the drink, and I say drink, as I like my kamikazes in a full glass and not some stupid shot glass. When I say small pinch, I mean about half a teaspoon, depending on what you're working with; if you're not familiar with the dose of the drug, you should not be doing it. Drink.

Peachy Keen Man

In a blender, combine an eighth of finely ground and deseeded marijuana, a couple psychedelic mushrooms, a shot of light rum, a shot of coconut rum, a shot of peach schnapps, a shot of 151, a few scoops of vanilla ice cream, a small shot of pineapple juice and a few shots of peach juice or nectar. Fill with some ice and blend with fresh peach; if not strong enough, float 151 on top of each portion. Garnish with whipped cream and a wedge of peach; mind peach pit.

Gangsta Grape Gonzo

In a blender, combine a handful or so of fresh seedless grapes with a quarter of finely ground seedless marijuana, two cups of grape flavored Mad Dog 20/20, three shots of 151 and as many grape flavored frozen freezer pops as you can fit in the blender with three scoops of vanilla ice cream.

Fresh Strawberry Frenzy

Take the tops off of some fresh strawberries, and put a handful or two of the berries into a blender. Add a tablespoon of sugar, two tablespoons of cream cheese, an eighth of psychedelic mushrooms, a shot of vanilla vodka, a shot of Bailey's, a shot of white chocolate liquor and some ice, then blend. Ice cream can be substituted instead of cream cheese and sugar.

Creamy Spiked Chocolate

Fill a blender with ice, an eighth of psychedelic mushrooms, a shot of Bailey's, a shot of Van Gogh chocolate vodka, a shot of crème de cacao, a shot of Godiva chocolate liquor, a splash of cream or skim milk and a squirt of chocolate syrup. If you're feeling indulgent, throw in a scoop of ice cream. Instead of cream or milk, you can use chocolate or vanilla soy milk. For another kind of low fat creaminess, try adding plain, vanilla or chocolate yogurt. For a brownie flavor, add a shot of amaretto or hazel nut flavored liquor. For crunch with the mushrooms, add some peanuts. Blending in a banana is good, too.

Colada Collision Course

In a blender, combine one small can of pineapple chunks in juice, one small can of coconut milk, a shot of coconut rum, a shot of 151, an eighth of psychedelic mushrooms or ground marijuana, three scoops of vanilla ice cream, a shot of Bailey's and some ice. For a twist, you can use coffee flavored liquor instead of Bailey's. You can also leave the Bailey's out all together and simply add some more coconut rum. Fresh coconut flakes are a nice add in to hide the texture of the mushrooms or marijuana. A banana is another great thing to consider adding into the mixer.

Special Spanish Rice

In a large pot, combine two cups of brown rice with a dab of hash butter and four cups of water. While the rice cooks, clean up an eighth of marijuana; de-stem and deseed it, then slowly mix it in with a couple psychedelic mushrooms, a dash of Italian seasoning, one small red pepper, one diced jalapeno pepper, one diced garlic clove and a large freshly diced tomato – in a bind, you can also use a can of tomato with garlic and onion mixed in it. Fresh Vidalia or sweet onion is best to add to the mix, though red onion can also be used, diced up. Stir frequently towards the end to prevent scorching the rice, and serve with chicken or whatever.

Fresh Bud Salad

Popcorn or bubblegum marijuana buds work best for this, but basically find some nice buds and tear the actual buds off the stems, leaving it in sticky chunks as the base of the salad, but layer these on top of a few fresh marijuana leaves at the bottom of the plate. Dice up whatever fresh berries are available, such as strawberries, blueberries, black berries, raspberries, or use dry cranberries. Throw on a handful of Garbanzo beans, crumbled hardboiled egg, chunks of ham, turkey or bacon, shredded carrots, sliced cucumber, a handful of sweet corn, alfalfa sprouts, bean sprouts, banana chunks, orange slices, almond slivers, pine nuts, black pepper, a squirt of lemon juice and dressing.

Maryjae's Mashed Potatoes

Peel and cut up half a pot full of potatoes, then boil until soft; for skin-on mashed potatoes, use the redskins and clean thoroughly. Potatoes are done when you can easily slide a fork through them. Drain the water and put into a large mixing bowl, adding a splash of milk, one third of a cup of hemp or mushroom butter, a pinch or two of finely ground marijuana, a dash or two of black pepper and a tiny dash of Cajun. Try half of a packet of dry ranch dressing instead of Cajun seasoning – or for cheesy garlic, finely dice a garlic clove and add a cup of shredded Colby jack cheese.

Hemp Steamed Veggies

Prepare your favorite vegetables to steam, such as broccoli and baby carrots, yellow squash and asparagus, red pepper and cauliflower, onion and green pepper with psychedelic mushrooms, zucchini and green beans, corn and cabbage, or any combination of the above or home-style favorites you have. Wash, cut and prepare veggies as normal, steaming them or putting them in a pan, but either way, top generously with hemp butter, Cajun seasoning, Italian seasoning, black pepper and a few pinches of freshly ground, deseeded and de-stemmed, marijuana.

Rhubarb Pot Pie

Acquire two 9-inch pie crusts, and layer one into a pie tin, molding it. Cut up one-inch chunks of rhubarb (about three full stalks) and combine it with two cups of either fresh strawberries or diced Granny Smith apples – if using apples, add a dash of cinnamon. Add in an eighth of bubblegum marijuana chunks, pulled from the stem and deseed but left into tiny chunks, dust powder sugar, light glaze maple syrup, tiny chunks of hash butter, a handful of fresh blueberries and a bit of raisins. Place the other crust on top and bake either according to package or at 375 for twenty five minutes or until crust is golden brown.

Buddy Fruit Salad

Layer fresh marijuana leaves on the bottom, and break up about an eighth of fresh marijuana bubblegum buds, pulling the buds off the stems, making sure there are no seeds, but keeping most of it in bud form, though saving the shake to toss on as topping later. Slice up kiwi fruit, banana musk melon, honey dew melon, watermelon, and add in a small can of mandarin oranges and a small can of pineapple chunks. For an added bonus, toss in a few psychedelic mushrooms, or for a little extra style, garnish with whipped cream or a variety of fresh berries.

BBQ Bud Veggies

For however many people are eating, tear off a good square of aluminum foil, as this is going to be rolled into a pouch that can be set directly onto a grill to cook along with any other grill foods. Peel fresh buds off of the stems, getting out any seeds and break into tiny chunks, saving the shake to use as a cooking herb later. Portion this out onto each foil, along with diced onion, green pepper, red pepper, garlic clove, broccoli, asparagus, celery, potatoes, corn, green beans or any other grilling vegetable. You can also add banana chunks and orange slices for a tropical twist. Sprinkle with Cajun and Italian.

Jello Bud Mold

Prepare an eighth of fresh buds, pulling the buds off the stems and making sure there are no seeds, leaving the buds in shaky chunks. Prepare your choice of fruit, which results in about two cups. For the texture of the buds, black berries work well to hide this. Blueberries, raspberries and strawberries also work well, but try to work with the flavor of Jello you have, using pineapple, banana, mandarin oranges or whatever best complements it. Prepare Jello as normal, or feel free to add in a cup of cold vanilla vodka instead of cold water, mix in the fruit and dump this into a bunt pan mold or bowl to chill.

Hidden Layer Cake

Prepare a yellow or chocolate cake according to recipe, so there results in two cakes to be layered. Using two cups of marshmallow cream, add up to an eighth of either ground marijuana or psychedelic mushrooms, a quarter cup to a half cup of coconut and a quarter cup to a half cup of chocolate chips. Generously coat the top of one cake with this concoction and place the other cake on top. Frost as normal using vanilla with chocolate chip frosting (or whipped cream to be lower in fat) and perhaps another sprinkle of mushrooms or pot, then decorate with coconut and miniature marshmallows. Food coloring can also be used.

Filet Hemp Stew

Dice up a garlic clove, a Vidalia onion, a green pepper, a red pepper, celery, a few psychedelic mushrooms and put it into a large pot. Pre-cook the vegetables for a minute with a generous dab of hemp butter, and cut up a couple filet mignons into bite sizes. Singe the outside of the meat. Add in a small can of green beans, a small can of corn, a small can of water chestnuts and can of peas. Broccoli, asparagus and cauliflower are optional additions, as are potatoes, either reds or can. Add about four cans of beef broth. Dump in a cup or two of ABC noodles, egg noodles, elbow noodles or homemade noodles. Season with Tony's, a beef bouillon cube, marjoram, Cajun seasoning, Italian seasoning, dill, freshly ground black pepper, some crushed red pepper (optional) and a fresh bay leaf, making sure to pull the leaf out before serving. For a cheeseburger styled stew, use only two cans of beef bouillon, and dump in a jar of cheese sauce; you can also use a milk or cream base, adding powdered cheese mix, or you can dissolve four tablespoons of cream cheese, a small container of sour cream, a small container of cream cheese, mixing in shredded sharp cheddar cheese and provolone, but potatoes should be used when using this method. Turn heat down to low and let simmer for a while; the longer it cooks, the more the flavors tend to come together.

Crusty Cashew Chew

In a bowl, mix an egg with a splash of milk, a half cup of crushed cashews and a few sprinkles of ground marijuana. Dunk either a fish filet such as salmon or tilapia in this mix, or you can you chicken alternately. In a skillet, green onions, peas, psychedelic mushrooms, three tablespoons of cream cheese, five tablespoons of hemp butter, a splash of white wine, a dash of Old Bay, a dash of white pepper, a dash of Italian seasoning cook. Add the cashew crusted filet to the already hot pan, cooking until done and garnishing with a sprinkle of ground marijuana and fresh parsley; serve over noodles.

Spinach Pasta Sizzler

Bring a large pot of water to boil with a pinch of sea salt and a dab of hemp butter to prepare some penne pasta. While doing that, prepare a skillet with your choice of meat: either sausage or chicken with just a couple hunks of bacon to flavor. You can also do this vegetarian. Add into the skillet freshly diced onion, green pepper, psychedelic mushrooms, a few de-stemmed and deseeded marijuana chunks, red pepper (jalapeno is optional), garlic, artichoke hearts and a generous handful of freshly washed spinach leaves or a small container of frozen spinach. Melt in a tablespoon of cream cheese. Add a large can of diced tomatoes with basil and oregano, ground pot, a pinch of rosemary, a pinch of thyme, dash marjoram, a pinch of red pepper and freshly ground black pepper. Just before combining the pasta with the sauce, cut up chunks of mozzarella cheese and toss in with some crumbled feta cheese, topping with parmesan cheese when serving.

Psychedelic Stuff Shrooms

In a broiler dish, prepare a bed of psychedelic mushrooms and a few generous chunks of hash butter, evenly distributed, to melt later. Fill the dish with chunks of crab and shrimp, mixed with confetti styled cut green and red peppers, freshly diced garlic, dashes of Old Bay and Italian seasoning; broil.

Hemp Chicken Salad

Layer each serving plate with fresh marijuana leaves. Using previously cooked either shredded or chunks of chicken, mix in one third cup of mayonnaise, one third cup of white wine Dijon mustard, a handful of cranberries (raisins or blueberries can be used instead), a handful of fresh grapes cut in halves or quarters (fresh cherries can be used instead), one third cup of crushed walnuts, a quarter cup of shredded carrots, a handful of celery chunks and a handful of cucumber chunks is optional. Mix in up to an eighth of ground marijuana and/or psychedelic mushrooms with a dash of ground black pepper, basil and dill.

Fry Me Potatoes

Shred a good amount of potatoes, how much depends on the number of people and how much you'll expect to eat, and put into a skillet with one third cup of hash butter, a few diced psychedelic mushrooms, diced garlic, diced green peppers, diced onions, a dash of paprika, a dash of black pepper, a dash of Italian seasoning and a dash of Cajun seasoning. Try a dash of sherry for flavoring. Instead of using ketchup, try using a fresh tomato, diced up and added just before it is taken out of the pan; for a kick try crushed red pepper or a dash of your favorite hot sauce, such as Dave's Insanity, Tabasco or Louisiana.

A Final Thought

Use this book as merely a guide to make your own creations, as that's what cooking is, an experiment. Look for the tricks, like using mayonnaise or apple sauce instead of oil, even in a cake if you can believe it, with nobody ever able to tell the difference... usually. Let inspiration take you where it may, as I did in writing this book between 11:02 p.m. May 29th and 2:36 a.m. on June 1st in 2007.

Cheers to all!

Marisa L. Williams
www.lulu.com/thorisaz

About The Author

Marisa Williams is the author of fifty independent books that range from cooking to music journalism, photography, novels, screenplays and even a children's book, amongst other things. Currently working on her thesis for Johns Hopkins University's graduate writing program in fiction, she toured as a Harley girl on Ozzfest in 2002 after beginning entertainment journalism in 2000, something she never thought she'd do, having a Bachelor of Science in forensics, especially since her temporarily paralyzing cliff diving accident in 1999. In 2006, five of her books were censored and pulled from publication, but the trend began in 2004, when novel "Heidi" was barred from publication.

More Foods and Thoughts

I know, this should have been the end of the book and all, but why not put the author information in the middle; after all, it is the Stoney Cook Book. I went to turn this into a book, just as is, but then I thought that there simply was not enough stuff – so here's a little more to keep you going.

These are some modified favorites. See, I began to think just how easy it was to substitute a little stoniness, so I fingered through a few more things hidden deep in the depths of my cooking folder, just to spice things up a bit. Hope they make you happy ;-)

My grandmother actually came to me for a few recipes, as she was sick of taking her pain medication. Of course, I got kidney stones from taking so many pills after my cliff diving accident, so I know how she feels. I guess what I'm saying is that there actually is a good side to the green, besides fiber I mean, so why not try to give the people as much as I can, right?

I'd feel bad putting out a book with just a few recipes, as it'd almost be like a waste of time, so the more the merrier. Usually, I'd say puff puff pass, but this time, we'll go with the more traditional dinner table passing. Just think of me cooking for my grandma; doesn't it give you the warm and fuzzies?

Now, I don't suggest serving this to your kids, unless you're like my grandma's age and your kids damn well know what it is that they're eating. I will suggest a slightly modified chai tea to set your mood straight. I might even suggest sipping that tea while chilling by a body of water, soaking up some rays and just relaxing.

Hazy Guacamole

Finely chop a small red onion and a few choice ripe weed buds, and in a large bowl, add a dash of key lime juice and garlic sea salt. Allow this to sit while you cut four large ripe avocados in half, taking out the pits. Scoop the avocado out of its skin, and mash it into the onion mix with a fork or potato masher. Stir in a finely diced tomato and a finely dice jalapeno pepper (in a hurry, you can add a can of diced tomatoes with either jalapeno or chilies already added into it), along with a few stalks of freshly chopped cilantro. You may like to let this refrigerate overnight before serving with tortilla chips.

Mango My Salsa

In a decent-sized bowl, toss together the
following: two diced tomatoes, a few finely
ripened weed buds, a ripe mango, a small finely
chopped onion, a few stalks of fresh cilantro, a
finely diced jalapeno, a tablespoon of orange
juice and a small dash of garlic sea salt. Some
may like it to be refrigerated (up to six hours)
before serving with tortilla chips or on top of
tacos, burritos, etc.

Strawberry Shortcake's High

For your base and middle, you can use either
sliced pound cake, angel food cake or traditional
shortcake cups. On top of your base, layer fresh
weed leaves, topped with fresh strawberry
chunks, pudding (either cheesecake, vanilla,
banana or your choice flavor – you can also add
in some finely ground weed or magic mushrooms
into your pudding if you like). Start the second
layer with your middle cake, more fresh
marijuana leaves, more strawberry chunks, more
pudding if you'd like and whipped cream. Top
with a fresh popcorn bud of marijuana and drizzle
with chocolate if you'd so desire.

Buddy Carrot Cake

Grease and flour two 8 or 9-inch baking pans; set aside. In a large mixing bowl, combine two cups flour, one and three-quarter cups of sugar, a tablespoon of cinnamon, a teaspoon of baking powder, a teaspoon of baking soda, a half teaspoon of salt, a half teaspoon of ground allspice and three tablespoons of ground marijuana (or magic mushrooms). Add one and a quarter cups of shredded carrots, an 8-oz can of crushed pineapple in its juice, three quarter cups of hash butter and four eggs. Beat on medium for a couple minutes, then stir in a cup of chopped walnuts by hand. Pour the batter into the prepared pans, and bake at 350 for 30 to 35 minutes or until a toothpick inserted near the center comes out clean. Top with cream cheese frosting, which is made by beating 8 oz of softened cream cheese in a large mixing bowl with a half cup of softened hash or mushroom butter and two teaspoons of vanilla. Mix with electric mixer until soft and fluffy, then gradually beat in about four cups of powdered sugar (enough so the frosting will be spreading consistency).

Psychedelic Lake Perch

Marinate six Lake Perch fillets (you can also use cod or flounder, even mahi-mahi) in a mixture of the following. A cup of buttermilk, a tablespoon of fresh parsley, two tablespoons of chives, a teaspoon of minced shallot, a teaspoon of diced garlic, three teaspoons of ground marijuana or magic mushrooms, a half teaspoon of sea salt and a half teaspoon of white pepper; let sit over night in fridge. Sautee the fillets with a quarter cup of hash or mushroom butter, a quarter cup of white wine, a dash of ground marijuana, a dash of Cajun seasoning, a handful of fresh buds and a handful of fresh magic mushrooms. Capers or fresh baby sweet peas also make great add-ins.

High-On Puffs

Preheat oven to 450 degrees, and grease a six-cup muffin or popover pan. In a medium mixing bowl, mix together a cup of flour with a half teaspoon of ground garlic sea salt, three tablespoons of ground marijuana and a half cup of Parmesan cheese (a half cup of finely diced green onion is optional). Whisk in two eggs and a cup of milk. Divide the batter amongst the cups, filing each about half. Bake for 15 minutes, reduce the heat to 350 and bake for another 20 minutes, making sure not to open the oven door while it bakes. Serve immediately smothered in hash or mushroom butter.

Spiced-Up Pumpkin Custard

In a mixing bowl, combine a 15 oz can of solid-pack pumpkin, two eggs, a cup of half-and-half, two-thirds cup packed brown sugar, one and a half teaspoons of pumpkin pie spice, a half teaspoon of salt and three tablespoons of ground marijuana. Beat until smooth, then pour into four greased 10 oz custard cups. Place in a two-inch deep baking pan, pouring hot water around the cups (about an inch deep). Bake for 20 minutes at 350. Meanwhile, combine a quarter cup of packed brown sugar, a quarter cup of chopped pecans and a tablespoon of melted hash or mushroom butter in a small bowl. Sprinkle over the custard and bake a half hour longer, until a knife inserted near the center comes out clean. Serve warm or chilled, topped with whipped cream, ground cinnamon and a fresh popcorn marijuana bud.

Who Spiked My Shrimp?

Combine a pound of peeled and de-veined large shrimp in a bowl with a quarter cup of key lime juice and tablespoon of melted hash butter, tossing to coat. Set aside. Melt a half cup of magic mushroom butter in a large skillet, adding two chopped green onions and three minced garlic cloves; sauté a couple minutes, then add the shrimp. Add a quarter cup of white wine, a pinch of cayenne pepper, three tablespoons of ground marijuana and a splash of lime. Simmer three to five minutes. For a side dish, slice up zucchini, fresh marijuana buds and red bell peppers. Sauté in hash butter with dashes of ground marijuana, garlic sea salt, Cajun seasoning and garlic pepper. To round off the meal, slice a loaf of French bread lengthwise, coating the interior with hash butter, parmesan cheese, diced tomatoes, chopped green onions and sprinkles of garlic sea salt, garlic pepper, sweet basil, dill and ground marijuana. Slice some mozzarella, topping off the inside of the bread, then put the two halves back together, wrap the bread in tin foil and bake for ten minutes at 400 (or throw on the grill for a couple minutes on each side).

Cheesy Apple High

Preheat oven to 375. Line a pie plate with one cruse, gently pressing dough amongst the edges, letting excess hang. In a large bowl, combine three pounds of Granny Smith apples, peeled and cut into chunks, with a third cup of flour, three quarter cups of sugar, a teaspoon of ground cinnamon, a quarter teaspoon of nutmeg, a tablespoon of lemon juice, a teaspoon of vanilla, a quarter teaspoon of salt and three tablespoons of ground marijuana. Spoon into pie crust and scatter bits of mushroom butter (about a couple tablespoons total) throughout. Top with an even layer of extra sharp cheddar cheese (about three ounces). Drape the second crust loosely over the filling, pulling the excess from the top and bottom crusts together to form an edge decoratively. Brush the top crust lightly with a beaten egg and make a few half-inch slits in the crust. Bake until the top is golden brown and the filling bubbles, fruit tender, about 53 minutes. Cool 15 minutes and serve.

Apple Rhubarb Munchie Bread

Heat oven to 350, and grease the bottom of two loaf pans. Mix a cup and a half of finely chopped rhubarb, a cup and a half of chopped Granny Smith apples, a cup and a half of sugar, a half cup of hash butter (melted), a teaspoon of vanilla and four eggs in a bowl. Stir in three cups of flour, a cup of chopped nuts, three and a half teaspoons of baking powder, a few tablespoons of ground marijuana, a teaspoon of cinnamon (teaspoon chai spice optional), and a teaspoon of salt (you can also add in a few finely chopped psychedelic mushrooms). Bake about an hour (perhaps 50 minutes, depending on oven).

Make Me Feel Like Molasses Cookies

Melt a half cup of hash butter and a quarter cup of mushroom butter and cool. Add a cup of sugar, a quarter cup of molasses and one egg. Beat well. Sift two cups of flour, two teaspoons of baking soda, a quarter teaspoon of salt, a half teaspoon of clove, a teaspoon of cinnamon and a half teaspoon of ginger. Roll in white sugar on a greased cookie sheet, then bake at 375 about ten minutes.

Crazy Cajun Lasagna

Preheat oven to 375, and cook a pound of lasagna noodles according to package; drain and rinse. Combine a pound of sausage and a pound of boneless, skinless cubed chicken with a dash of sage, an eighth of deseeded ground marijuana and a couple dashes of Cajun seasoning; cook in a large skillet with a couple stalks of chopped celery, one small chopped onion, a handful of chopped psychedelic mushrooms, one chopped green pepper and a clove of finely chopped garlic. When meat is done, stir in a 10 oz container of Alfredo sauce and a half cup of parmesan cheese. Lightly coat the bottom of baking dish with hash butter, layering noodles, followed by the meat sauce mixture and generous sprinkles of shredded mozzarella cheese; repeat layers until out of ingredients, then coat the top generously with mozzarella. Bake for an hour and let stand about 15 minutes before serving.

Seeing Twirls Tortellini

Preheat oven to 400. Cook two 8 oz packages of cheese-filled tortellini according to directions; drain and set aside. In a medium saucepan, cook a finely diced red onion and a couple tablespoons of finely chopped shallots in a tablespoon of hash butter until tender. Stir in two cups of half-and-half and a half cup of milk, bringing it to a boil, then remove from heat. In a small bowl, beat a couple egg yolks, and slowly add a cup of the hot mix to it, beating until combined. Return all to saucepan, cooking over medium low heat about ten minutes, thickening until slightly bubbly. Stir in a third cup of parmesan cheese, a teaspoon of Italian seasoning, one third cup of ground marijuana and a dash of pepper. Transfer half the noodles to a baking dish, then coat with a half cup of finely shredded Gruyere cheese and a half cup of finely diced psychedelic mushrooms; top with remaining noodles, a couple of ounces of prosciutto or finely chopped and cooked ham, then cover with the sauce. Top with a half cup of walnut pieces and a half cup of shredded mozzarella. Bake for 20 minutes until top is lightly browned, mix bubbling. Let stand for 15 minutes; serve.

Confusion Crab Cakes

In a skillet, heat a tablespoon of hash butter six thinly sliced scallions, a clove of minced garlic and a chopped green pepper; cook until soft (about four minutes). In a large bowl, combine five tablespoons of mayonnaise, a third cup of heavy cream, three tablespoons of Dijon mustard, a dash of garlic sea salt, a quarter cup of finely ground marijuana, a quarter cup of finely diced magic mushrooms, a dash of garlic pepper, a small dash of cayenne pepper, two eggs, a pinch of parsley and a quarter cup of lemon juice. Mix in sautéed vegetables and 30 saltine crackers, crumbled finely. Rest for a few minutes, then form the mix into two to three-inch wide patties, about an inch high, resting the patties on wax paper until ready to cook. Heat a skillet with two tablespoons of hash butter over medium low heat. Sauté the cakes for about five minutes on each side or until golden brown (don't try to cook them all at once by forcing them into the pan). Blot excess grease.

Psychedelic Zucchini Bread

Heat oven to 350; grease and flour two loaf pans. In a large bowl, beat three eggs, two cups of sugar, a cup of hash butter (melted) and a teaspoon of vanilla until smooth, then beat in 8 oz of cream cheese (softened). In another large bowl, whisk two cups of lour, a teaspoon of baking soda, a teaspoon of baking powder, a teaspoon of cinnamon, a teaspoon of salt, a half teaspoon of nutmeg and three tablespoons of ground psychedelic mushrooms or pot. Gradually beat this into egg mix. Fold in two cups of chopped walnuts and two cups of shredded zucchini. Raisins and chocolate chips make interesting add-ins (about a cup of either or both), but they are optional. Divide the batter between the loaf pans, baking at 350 for an hour or until a toothpick inserted in the center comes out clean.

Tropical Dream Cake

Preheat oven to 350; grease and flour two 9-inch cake pans. In a large bowl, whisk together three cups of flour, a teaspoon of baking soda, a teaspoon of salt, two cups of sugar, a teaspoon of cinnamon and a quarter cup of finely ground marijuana. Add three large lightly beaten eggs and three quarter cups of hash butter (melted). Stir in a cup of chopped pecans, two large mashed bananas, a teaspoon and a half of vanilla and an 8 oz can of crushed pineapple in its juice. Bake for 28 minutes or until toothpick inserted into center comes out clean. For frosting, beat 8 oz of softened cream cheese in a large bowl with a half cup of softened psychedelic mushroom butter (or has butter), a 16 oz box of confectioners' sugar and a teaspoon of vanilla.

Crazy Coffee Cake (enough to share)

Mix yeast, a half cup of milk, three tablespoons of sugar and a tablespoon of flour; let stand in a warm spot until is starts to rise. Heat a quart of milk. Add a pound of hash butter, a pound of psychedelic mushroom butter and three cups of sugar. In a separate bowl, mix ten egg whites till foamy. Mix in all the yokes of 20 eggs. Add three cups of sour cream, a teaspoon of brandy, a half teaspoon of almond flavor, a teaspoon of rum, a tablespoon of vanilla, a quarter teaspoon of yellow food coloring and a tablespoon of salt. Beat well. Blend mixtures and add ten pounds of flour. Next add the yeast mixture and beat well. Let it rise and make loaves. Brush on a mixture of one egg, one egg white, a quarter teaspoon of yellow coloring and a teaspoon of sugar. Bake at 325 for 40-45 minutes, using toothpick to determine if done. For shinny tops brush on a thick mixture of a half cup of strong tea and three tablespoons of sugar. For poppy seed cake, mix in a can of poppy seed, a cup of powdered sugar and a tablespoon of honey, mixed well and folded into the bread mix.

Chocolate Creeper Pie

Heat oven to 350. Melt two ounces of unsweetened chocolate, dividing it between the bottoms of two pie crusts. Top with a half cup of pecans on each pie. In a large mixing bowl, beat 3 oz of cream cheese, a half cup of hash butter and four eggs. In a separate mixing bowl, whisk a cup and a half of sugar, a half cup of cocoa, a tablespoon of flour, a small dash of salt and a quarter cup of finely ground and deseeded marijuana. Beat into egg mixture. Slowly beat in a 12 oz can of evaporated milk. Add a quarter cup of brandy and beat for five minutes. Divide the mixture in half, pouring about two and a half cups into each pie shell. Bake for 35 minutes or until center is set. Cool completely. Garnish with whipped cream and chocolate curls.

Cornball Muffins

Preheat oven to 375. Grease 12 muffin pans. In a large bowl, mix a cup and a half of flour, a cup of cornmeal, a half cup of sugar, a tablespoon of baking powder and three quarter teaspoon of salt. Stir in a half cup of hash butter, melted, until blended. In a small bowl, whisk two large eggs, three quarter cups of milk, two tablespoons honey and two tablespoons maple syrup. Combine flour mixture with egg mixture (batter will be lumpy). Spoon batter into muffin cups. Bake for 20 minutes or until toothpick comes out clean when inserted into center.

Tomato Haze Soup

Strain a can of chopped tomatoes, reserving the juice, and spread onto a baking sheet, seasoning with pepper and garlic sea salt. Drizzle a quarter cup of melted hash butter and roast until caramelized, about 15 minutes at 450. In a saucepan, heat a half cup of hash butter with two stalks of diced celery, two diced carrots, a diced onion, and two finely chopped garlic cloves, cooking about ten minutes until soft. Add the tomatoes, the reserved juice, a can of chicken broth, a bay leaf and two tablespoons of psychedelic mushroom butter. Simmer until vegetables are very tender, about 20 minutes. Add a dash of basil, a dash of ground marijuana and a half cup of heavy cream.

Seventh Heaven Sweet Potatoes

Preheat oven to 400. Wrap each sweet potato (six is a good number to start with) in tin foil, drizzle with hash butter and wrap tightly. Bake on a cookie sheet, turning once, until very tender, about an hour. Cool and carefully unwrap the potatoes. Cut each in half and scoop out the flesh into a bowl, discard skins. Mash with two tablespoons of maple syrup and two tablespoons of apple cider vinegar until smooth; dash with garlic sea salt, ground marijuana and pepper. Transfer into a serving bowl, topping with two tablespoons of hash butter (cut up into pieces) and a quarter cup of pecan halves.

Caramelize My Brain Cake

Preheat oven to 350. Grease two-quart square baking dish. Arrange two Granny Smith apples, peeled and thinly sliced, in the bottom of dish; sprinkle with lemon juice, a half teaspoon of cinnamon, one-eighth of a teaspoon of nutmeg and top evenly with a quarter cup of raisins. Set aside. In a large mixing bowl, stir together a cup of flour, three quarter cups of packed brown sugar, a teaspoon of baking powder, a quarter teaspoon of baking soda and a quarter cup of ground marijuana, deseeded. Add a half cup of milk, two teaspoons of psychedelic mushroom butter and a teaspoon of vanilla; mix well. Stir in a half cup of chopped pecans. Spread the batter evenly over apples. In a small saucepan, combine three quarter cups of caramel topping, a half cup of water, and a tablespoon of hash butter, bringing it to boil. Pour this over the batter in the baking dish. Bake for 35 minutes. While warm, cut into pieces, inverting each piece onto dessert dish and spooning the caramel apple mix from the bottom of the pan over each piece. Serve with whipped cream.

Cocoa Quake Cake

Allow a half cup of hash butter, two eggs and three egg whites to sit at room temperature for a half hour. Grease and lightly flour two 6-cup fluted tube pans. In a medium bowl, mix one and one third cup of flour, a half cup of cocoa, a quarter teaspoon of baking powder, a quarter teaspoon of baking soda, a quarter teaspoon of salt and a quarter cup of finely ground and deseeded marijuana. In a small bowl, dissolve two tablespoons dissolve instant chai tea into two tablespoons of hot water, stirring in one and a half teaspoons of vanilla; set aside. In a large mixing bowl, beat hash butter with an electric mixer on medium for 30 seconds. Gradually add two cups of sugar, a half cup of sour cream, eggs and egg whites. Alternately beat flour mix and chai mix into butter mix, beating on low speed. Stir in five and a half ounces of chopped bittersweet chocolate. Pour into pan. Bake for 35 minutes or until a toothpick comes out clean from center. Cook for 15 minutes. Sprinkle with powdered sugar before serving.

My Bottom is Fudge Pie

For the crust, in a bowl, mix a cup of graham cracker crumbs, two tablespoons confectioners' sugar and three and a half tablespoons of hash butter. Press evenly over bottom and sides of 9-inch pie plate. Place pan in freezer. For bottom, in a medium bowl, place a half pound of bittersweet chocolate, finely chopped, along with a quarter cup of finely ground and deseeded marijuana. In a small saucepan, heat a cup of heavy cream until small bubbles appear around edges. Pour over chocolate, allowing it to stand for five minutes, then whisk until smooth. Remove crust from freezer, pouring chocolate into crust, and refrigerate for an hour until firm. For filling, in a large bowl, mix two cups of heavy cream and two cups of light cream with two 3.4 oz packets of instant vanilla pudding mix.

Beat on high until peaks form. Spoon over chocolate layer, then place in freezer until frozen, about 4 or 5 hours. To serve, allow to partially thaw in refrigerator, garnish with chocolate shavings and slice.

Makes Me Clammy Chowder

You can use two pounds of clam, scrubbing them well, soaking in water with a handful of flour (or cornmeal to help eliminate sand) for a half our before draining them and boiling them until the shells open, or you can use a pound of shelled or canned clams (or canned mussels or cockles instead). If you do boil the clams, reserve the water. Cook up three ounces of diced bacon, until the fat is rendered, browning the bacon. Add in a large diced onion and some diced up green onions, a few stalks of celery, either a sweet yellow pepper (finely diced) or some shallots, a tablespoon of flour, a pinch a garlic sea salt, a pinch of white pepper, a quarter cup of ground marijuana, a quarter cup of psychedelic mushrooms (finely diced), four cups of milk, the reserved clam juice and six medium cubed potatoes. Cover and bring to boil, cooking for about ten minutes until potatoes are nearly tender. Remove the calms from their shells if you need to, dicing up any large pieces if desired. Add a cup of light cream, some chopped parsley and another cup of milk, cooking until the potatoes and clams are tender. Serve immediately.

Barbeque Me Wine-o Sauce

In a large bowl, combine the following ingredients to use as a sauce or marinade for pork, seafood or chicken (or get creative): a half cup of balsamic vinegar, a large finely chopped shallot, three minced garlic cloves, a 15 oz can of tomato sauce, two tablespoons of white wine Dijon mustard, two tablespoons of molasses, a tablespoon of honey, a quarter cup of ground and deseeded marijuana, a large pinch of white pepper, a dash of sea salt, three tablespoons of finely ground psychedelic mushrooms (you can also finely dice them if you prefer), an extremely finely diced red pepper, a pinch of mustard seed, a pinch of dill and a tiny splash of white wine.

Smiling Salmon Pate

You can use an 8 oz can of red or pink salmon drained, or fresh, removing any bones and skin.

Work the salmon into a smooth paste with the back of a spoon. Beat a half cup of low fat cottage cheese until it is smooth, adding this to the salmon, along with a few drops of key lime juice, a pinch of ground mace or nutmeg, a tiny dash of Tabasco sauce, a pinch of freshly ground garlic sea salt, a tablespoon of ground marijuana, a tablespoon of ground psychedelic mushrooms, a pinch of pepper and two tablespoons of low fat natural yogurt. When thoroughly incorporated, divide into four custard cups, smoothing the surfaces. Lay a fresh marijuana leaf on top of each cup. Using four small pickles, slice each lengthways four or five times, but do not cu through the gherkin at the narrow end, so you can splay the cut ends into a fan to use as decoration for the tops of the pates. Top each off with a fresh marijuana popcorn bud and a magic mushroom.

Make Me a Melon, Shrimp

Cut two small melons in half through the middle, removing the seeds. Scoop out the flesh with a melon baller, spoon or ice cream scoop. Leave a quarter inch of fruit on the inside of each shell. Peel four medium tomatoes, remove the seeds and cut the flesh into strips. Peel a cucumber and cube it. Peel and segment an orange. In a large bowl, mix together with the juice from half a lemon, four tablespoons of melted hash butter, three tablespoons of heavy cream. Stir in two tablespoons of fresh mint, three tablespoons of ground marijuana, a pinch of sugar, a dash of sea salt, a pinch of white pepper, a teaspoon of lemon thyme, a cup and a quarter of peeled and cooked shrimp and three quarter cups of slivered almonds (some shredded coconut also makes a great addition). Pile this mixture into the reserved shells and chill. Garnish with a mint leaf, a fresh marijuana leaf and a fresh marijuana popcorn bud.

Gratin-ny Haze?

Heat oven to 400. Coat a 3 and a half quart casserole with hash butter. In a medium both whisk together three eggs, two and a half cups buttermilk, a tablespoon of thyme, a half cup of hemp butter, a quarter pound of grated parmesan cheese, a pound of shredded pepper jack cheese (some use Swiss, but you can also mix mozzarella and feta together), two teaspoons sea salt, a pinch of pepper, a pinch of marjoram, a pinch of Cajun seasoning and a three tablespoons of ground marijuana; set aside. Arrange a layer of slightly overlapping potatoes (about two pounds cut up, or you can substitute a head of cauliflower, diced, for a real nice spin – or you can even mix the two) in the casserole. Cover with a layer of applies, about two pounds of cut up Granny Smiths, unpeeled. Pour over a third of the egg mixture, then make two more layers. Bake, covered, for an hour and 15 minutes. Remove cover and bake another 15 minutes or until potatoes (or cauliflower bits) are tender.

Ginger Chicken Daze Salad

Slice a boneless, skinless chicken breast and sauté it in hemp butter with a dash of soy sauce, a teaspoon of honey, a pinch of white pepper, a pinch of garlic sea salt, a dash of ginger, a tablespoon of orange juice, a dash of white wine, a few diced up psychedelic mushrooms, some sugar snow peas, a can of drained water chestnuts and a dash of ground marijuana. Prepare bowls of fresh marijuana leaves, decorating each salad with some mandarin orange slices, cherry tomatoes, almond slivers and a portion of chicken, mushrooms and peas. Top off with a sprinkle of grated parmesan cheese, some fresh popcorn marijuana buds and a couple extra psychedelic mushrooms. You can also toss all ingredients in a bowl and allow each person to serve themselves.

Dazed by Chocolate Cookies

Heat oven to 350. Coarsely chop a 16 oz package of semi-sweet baking chocolate (or use chips); set aside. Microwave another 16 oz package in a large microwaveable bow on high for a minute or two, being careful to stir it after a minute, reaching all the way to the bottom, because sometimes it doesn't look like the top is melted, but the bottom is, and too much can scorch it. When smooth, stir in three quarter cups of packed brown sugar, a quarter cup of hash butter, two eggs, and a teaspoon of vanilla. Stir in a half cup of flour, a quarter teaspoon of baking powder and two tablespoons of finely ground marijuana, deseeded, then add in the reserved chocolate chunks, along with two cups of chopped nuts (optional; you can also substitute raisins or coconut). Drop quarter cupfuls onto an ungreased cookie sheet, and bake for 12 minutes or until cookies are puffed and feel set to the touch.

Heady apple Caramel Cake

In a large saucepan, bring two cups of apple cider to boil. Cook until reduced to a half cup, about 20 minutes, then reduce head to medium high, stirring in a half cup of sugar, cooking about five minutes until sugar dissolves, stirring occasionally. Remove from heat and cool for a minute before stirring in a tablespoon of hash butter. Stir in three cups of peeled and sliced apples, like McIntosh, then cook for 15 minutes on medium high or until the liquid is absorbed, stirring frequently. Remove from heat. Preheat oven to 325. Coat a 12-cup bundt pan with hemp butter and dust with bread crumbs. In a large pan, combine a cup and half of sugar, a half cup of hash butter, a tablespoon of lemon rind and 8 oz of softened cream cheese, beating at medium speed for about five minutes. Add three large eggs, then beat in two tablespoons of lemon juice. Level three cups of flour and combine that with a half teaspoon of baking soda, a quarter teaspoon of salt and a tablespoon of ground marijuana. Add flour mix to sugar mix, alternately pouring a cup of butter milk. Fold in apple mixture and pour into prepared pan; bake at 325 for an hour and a half or until a toothpick comes out clean from the center. Combine a quarter cup of cider, a quarter cup of sugar, a quarter cup of lemon juice and a teaspoon of vanilla, stirring until sugar dissolves. Cool cake in pan for five minutes and pierce in several places, then pour the cider mix over the cake in pan and allow it to stand for ten minutes. Remove from pan, cool completely, then sprinkle with powdered sugar before serving.

Orange Poppy Cloud Bread

Beat three eggs, three quarter cups of sugar, one and a half cups of milk, and one and a half cups of melted hemp butter in a medium bowl. In another bowl, mix three cups of flour, one and a half teaspoons of salt, one and a half tablespoons of poppy seeds, two teaspoons of almond extract and a pinch of ground marijuana. Combine into batter, then pour into to greased loaf pans and bake for an hour. Put a toothpick in the center to ensure that it is done. To prepare glaze, mix one and a quarter cups of frozen orange juice concentrate with three quarter cups of powdered sugar, a teaspoon of almond extract and a quarter teaspoon of vanilla extract. When spreading consistency, pour mixture over hot loaves when they come out of the oven, allowing them to cool in pans.

Dreamy Zucchini Cookies

Combine a cup of zucchini, grated, with a teaspoon of baking soda, a cup of sugar, a half cup of hash butter and a beaten egg. Add two cups of flour, a teaspoon of cinnamon, a tablespoon of ground marijuana, a half teaspoon of cloves, a half teaspoon of salt, a cup of chopped walnuts and two teaspoons of vanilla. Chill for a couple hours. Drop by teaspoonful onto lightly greased cookie sheet and bake for 13 minutes at 375.

Peakin' Potato Pierogies

In a medium bowl, whisk a large egg and two heaping tablespoons of sour cream until smooth. Add a cup of milk and a cup of water. Add three cups of flour, stirring with a wooden spoon. Turn dough out onto a well-floured surface and work in about a cup of flour as you knead. Use a plastic scraper to lift dough, as it will stick to the counter before the flour is worked in. Knead about ten minutes, working in another half cup of flour until dough is elastic and no longer sticky. Place dough in a lightly floured bowl and set aside. Cook five pounds of peeled and cut baking potatoes in salted boiling water until fork tender, then drain and mash. Add four tablespoons of melted magic mushroom butter, a pound of melted hash butter, a half cup of grated cheddar cheese, 4 oz cream cheese, one small diced onion, a few slices of diced and cooked bacon, a few diced magic mushrooms, a dash of garlic sea salt, a dash of pepper and a dash of ground marijuana. Place a large pot of salted water on stove and bring to boil. Lay clean linen towel on counter and evenly distribute about two tablespoons of cornmeal to prevent sticking. On a floured surface, roll out dough to about one-eighth inch thickness and cut into two and a half inch circles. Form filling into one and a half inch balls, and place a ball in the center of each dough circle. Holding a circle in your hand, fold dough over filling and pinch the edges, forming a thoroughly sealed crescent. Transfer to linen towel. Continue until all circles are filled. (At this point, you can slather pierogies in hash butter and put in Ziplock bags to freeze, then fry in a skillet when ready with magic mushroom butter, or you can continue onward with the cooking process, or do a little of both, freeze some for later and cook some now). Add pierogi to the boiling water in batches. They will since to the bottom of the pot, then rise to the top. Once they rise, let them cooked for about a minute more. Meanwhile, drizzle platter with melted hemp butter. Remove pierogi from pot and transfer to platter to prevent sticking. Serve immediately.

Bake me like a Potato Salad

Fry up a cup of chopped bacon until crisp with a couple stalks of chopped celery, a few diced magic mushrooms and a chopped onion   Once cooked, add in three tablespoons of flour, a dash of sea salt, a dash of pepper and a dash of ground marijuana; cook for a couple minutes. Add two-thirds cup of sugar, two-thirds cup of apple cider vinegar, a cup and a half of water, stirring, and bring to boil to cook for two minutes. Add a third cup of fresh chopped parsley, a couple teaspoons of celery seed. Stir and remove from head. Preheat oven to 375. Place four pounds of boiled, peeled and sliced red skin potatoes in a 13-inch casserole dish, greased by hash butter, and pour the dressing over the potatoes, mixing gently. Bake 45 minutes or until the middle of the casserole bubbles and serve hot.

Loco Chicken enchiladas

Mix a can of cream of chicken soup with an 8 oz container of sour cream, a cup of Picante Sauce, a quarter cup of ground marijuana, and two teaspoons of chili powder. Mix one cup of this mix with one diced and cooked chicken breast (try cooking it in a pan with hash butter and a few diced up magic mushrooms) and a cup of pepper jack cheese. Using ten warmed soft tortilla shells, place a fresh marijuana leaf inside and spread about a quarter cup of the chicken mixture down the center of each tortilla. Roll up and place seam-side down in a baking dish. Pour remaining picante sauce mix over enchiladas. Top off with diced green onion, tomato, red pepper and a diced garlic clove. Cover and bake at 350 for 40 minutes.

A Real Pot Pie

Form a pie crust into a pie plate. Cook a pound of sausage (or a pound of chicken, or a half pound of each is really the way to go) with a diced onion, red pepper, a couple garlic cloves and about an eighth of marijuana leaves. Mix in a touch of Cajun seasoning, a pinch of marjoram and a tiny pinch of dill. When done, mix in a half cup of ricotta cheese, a half cup of feta cheese, a half cup of parmesan cheese, a cup of shredded mozzarella or pepper jack cheese and a couple eggs. Line the bottom of the pie with fresh marijuana leaves (remember, they'll shrink up when you cook them). Pour the meat mixture into the pie. Top off with cheese sprinkles and more fresh marijuana leaves, and form the second pie crust on top, making a few half-inch slits in it.

Cook at 375 for about an hour, until crust is golden brown.

Seafood Burritos, Totally Baked

In a bowl, mix 8 oz of cream cheese with a pound of seafood (crab, shrimp, crawdads or a combination – you could also do a half pound of seafood with a half pound of sausage, pre-cooked, for a Cajun feel, which is excellent), diced green onions, diced yellow sweet peppers, diced shallots, a quarter cup of feta cheese, a quarter cup of cheddar cheese, a quarter cup of pepper jack cheese, a dash of Old Bay, a dash of Cajun seasoning, a quarter cup of ground marijuana and a few diced psychedelic mushrooms. Using a package of soft tortilla shells, place a few fresh marijuana leaves in each shell, then spread about a quarter cup of the mixture into each shell, rolling each up and placing in a baking dish, seam-side down. Sprinkle the top with pepper jack and cheddar cheeses, a few sprinkles of ground marijuana and psychedelic mushrooms, another dash of Old Bay and another dash of Cajun, then bake for 20 minutes at 350.

Specially Stuffed Peppers

Cut off the tops and remove the insides of six large green peppers. In a skillet, cook a pound of sausage with a diced onion, a couple minced garlic cloves, a few stalks of chopped celery, a few diced magic mushrooms, a dash of sea salt, a quarter cup of ground marijuana, a dash of pepper and a small can of corn (or cut the kernels off of an ear of fresh sweet corn). Once cooked, mix in two cups of brown rice, a regular-sized can of drained black beans, and a cup of Monterey Jack cheese. Line the inside of each pepper with a couple fresh marijuana leaves, then pour in the meat and rice mixture; set each stuffed pepper standing up into a baking dish. Mix two cans of cream of mushroom soup with a can of diced tomatoes (or dice up a large fresh tomato), a few dashes of freshly ground marijuana and a dash of Cajun seasoning. Pour this mixture over the green peppers, and bake at 350 for 40 minutes.

Marijuana Leaf Balls

Fill a frying pan with fresh marijuana leaves and cook them down with three quarter cups of hash butter (or you can use the left over leaves from making hash butter for this recipe but make sure the leaves are extra buttery and still "wet"). Mix in some diced green onions, six eggs, a package of herb bread stuffing, a half cup of parmesan cheese, a dash of garlic powder, a dash of Italian seasoning, a dash of pepper; the mix will be thin. Refrigerate for several hours or overnight, then roll into one-inch balls (it's optional to then roll the balls in shredded mozzarella or sprinkle mozzarella on top of the balls before you bake them). Bake for 20 minutes at 350.

Marijuana Artichoke Dip

Combine a few handfuls of fresh marijuana leaves with a can of artichoke hearts (you can also use fresh artichoke diced up), an 8 oz package of cream cheese, a quarter cup of feta cheese, a quarter cup of ricotta cheese, a few diced magic mushrooms, a few diced slices of cooked bacon, a diced red onion, a diced red pepper, a few sliced garlic cloves, a dash of pepper, a dash of Cajun, a dash of Italian seasoning, a dash of dill, and a dash of marjoram. Top off with mozzarella cheese and bake at 350 for about 45 minutes. For an added delight, you can also stir-in your favorite seafood, such as shrimp, crab or crawdads, even de-boned salmon, but I would wait to add the seafood until after it has baked (cook the seafood while it bakes, using hash butter and Old Bay), then add it in, so as not to overcook the seafood. Serve either hot or cold with tortilla chips, crackers or baked bagel chips.

Marijuana Cheese Squares

Heat oven to 350 and grease a 13 x 9 pan with hemp butter. In a medium bowl, beat a couple eggs and add a cup of flour, a cup of milk, a quarter cup of melted hash butter, three cups of cubed or shredded Monterey Jack cheese, a few handfuls of fresh marijuana leaves, a teaspoon of baking powder, a pinch of garlic sea salt, a dash of chili powder and a few diced magic mushrooms, about 4 oz. Adding in pre-cooked ham, sausage or bacon bits are optional for flavor. Chicken can also be used, if so desired. Spread the mixture into prepared pan and bake for 35 to 40 minutes until golden brown. Let stand 10 minutes and cut into squares.

Totally Baked Macaroni

Cook a one pound package of elbow macaroni about three to five minutes less than package directs. Drain well. Preheat oven to 400 and grease a 13 x 9 pan with has butter. Spread a third of the pasta in the prepared dish. Sprinkle with a small amount of garlic sea salt, some pepper, ground marijuana and about a cup of shredded cheddar and Monterey Jack cheeses (a mixed blend of both). Dot with a tablespoon of hash butter. Repeat layers twice, pouring four cups of whole milk on top. Bake for 45 minutes.

Surprise Cabbage Casserole

Cook a pound of ground sausage with a diced onion, green pepper, a couple diced celery stalks, a handful of fresh marijuana leaves (or a quarter cup of ground marijuana), a dash of Italian seasoning and a couple minced garlic cloves. While this cooks, prepare two cups of rice, then mix the two together. Also cut up a head of cabbage into wedges and boil until tender, then chop up cabbage. Using a 4 quart casserole dish, pour some sauce from a small jar of spaghetti sauce into the bottom, then cover with the cabbage, a few fresh marijuana leaves, then the meat. Repeat the layers, pouring remaining sauce on top. Sprinkle with shredded cheddar cheese. Bake at 350 for an hour and let cool five minutes.

Marijuana Salmon Salad

Cook a filet of salmon with hash butter, a diced sweet pepper, chopped green onions, Cajun seasoning and Old Bay. Prepare a bowl of freshly picked marijuana leaves, decorating it with mandarin orange slices, cucumber slices and cherry tomatoes. Place the cooked and de-boned salmon on top with onions and peppers, using the left over hash butter drippings as dressing for the salad. Sprinkle with almond slivers and raisins.

Sloshy Shrimp Salad

Prepare a 10 oz package of bow ties pasta (about three cups but for more people, use a 16 oz package and really any shape of pasta works). Peel and de-vein a pound and a half of shrimp, cooking it with a few tablespoons of hash butter, a small diced red onion, a few stalks of diced celery, a diced sweet pepper, a quarter cup of ground marijuana, a few diced psychedelic mushrooms, a dash of Old Bay and a dash Cajun. Mix this with the pasta, including any left over hash butter, along with a cup of Italian dressing (or citrus vinaigrette), a diced tomato and about two oz of black olives (optional).

Marijuana Fruit Salad

Prepare serving bowls with fresh marijuana leaves. Into each bowl place some fresh blueberries, strawberries, watermelon balls (using juice as dressing or drizzle Brianna's Organic Poppy Seed Dressing), peach slices, pear slices and/or apple slices, raspberries or black berries. Top off with candied pecans or glazed almonds. Optional substitutions or additions include shredded coconut, raisins, dried cranberries, honey dew melon balls and mini-marshmallows.

I'm Fried Veal Chops

Rub veal chops with Italian seasoning, ground marijuana and pepper. In a large skillet, prepare three garlic cloves, minced, with three tablespoons of hash butter, and diced green onions. Just before you add the veil chops, throw in another tablespoon or so of hash butter. Fry up the veil chops. When they are done, sprinkle the pan lightly with key lime juice (or lemon, a couple tablespoons) and a couple tablespoons of water. Use a wooden spoon or plastic scraper to get up any browned bits from the bottom, and pour this pan juice over the veil when served.

Smoked Out Macaroni

Prepare large elbow pasta according to package. Preheat oven to 350. In a saucepan, cook a diced onion over medium-high heat with chicken broth, one can of reduced sodium, covered over medium heat for about five minutes. Mix a half teaspoon of dry mustard with a cup of half and half, a pinch of pepper, three tablespoons ground marijuana and a tablespoon of flour into the broth. Cook until just bubbly. Remove from heat, adding a half cup of smoked Gouda cheese and a half cup of cheddar cheese. Pour this sauce over pasta until combined, and put this into a casserole. Bake for 10 minutes covered, then another ten minutes uncovered. Let stand five minutes, then top with a medium chopped Granny Smith apple and a tablespoon of grated parmesan cheese. For an additional add-in, cook a boneless, skinless chicken breast in a pan with three tablespoons of hash butter and a few diced magic mushrooms, adding this to the mix before baking. Serve over fresh marijuana leaves.

The Fish Fried Me

Cut up a pound of sole or cod fillets into inch long strips after taking out all the bones. Roll these strips into a mix of flour, Old Bay, Cajun and ground marijuana, then dip them into a beaten egg and roll them in shredded coconut. Fry the fish in hash butter, adding a dash of ginger, finely chopped red chili, a small dash of chili powder, a pinch of ground marijuana, a few diced magic mushrooms, a pinch of ground nutmeg, a diced garlic clove. Finally, add a diced tomato, a couple dashes of soy sauce, a couple dashes of lemon juice, a tablespoon of water, a small pinch of brown sugar, ground garlic sea salt and a pinch of white pepper. Simmer a few minutes, then serve the fish, retaining the excess sauce to be handed out separately or drizzled over fresh marijuana leaves.

Crabbed me by the Balls

Mix a pound of crab meat, finely chopped with the crumbs from four slices of bread, crusts removed (you can also use shrimp or crawdads). Melt a tablespoon of hash butter, mixing in a tablespoon of flour. Stir in a half cup of milk, and bring to a boil, stirring constantly. Stir this into the crab meat and crumbs, adding a finely diced chili (you can use a red or green pepper instead), a few finely diced magic mushrooms, a dash of Old Bay, a dash of Cajun, a finely chopped green onion, a tablespoon of chopped parsley, a tablespoon of ground marijuana and a dash of garlic sea salt. Cover and cool completely. Shape the cold mix into balls, about one inch, with floured hands. Coat with beaten egg and dry bread crumbs. Fry in hash butter in a pan until golden brown, turning constantly. Drain on paper towels. Sprinkle with salt if desired. Serve each on a fresh marijuana leaf.

Drunken Chicken Stew

Coat a pound and a half of boneless, skinless chicken breasts, cubed, with a mixture of flour, garlic sea salt and ground marijuana, then cook in a pot with six tablespoons of hash butter, a minced garlic clove, finely chopped green onion, three medium diced carrots, a diced sweet pepper, a couple diced celery stalks and a few diced magic mushrooms. When chicken is no longer pink, add a bottle of white wine or champagne, two cans of fat free chicken broth, reduced sodium, a pinch of sea salt, a pinch of pepper, Italian seasoning, Cajun seasoning, and a pinch of ground marijuana. Bring to a boil, adding an 8 oz bag of wide noodles, cooking until noodles are soft. Stir in a couple tablespoons of minced parsley and a pinch of marjoram. You can also add in a can of black beans, corn or peas.

Jammin' Jokester Jambalaya

Melt two tablespoons of hash butter into a saucepan and add two tablespoons of flour. Stir to blend well and cook over low heat until a pale straw color. Add a diced onion, a few diced magic mushrooms, a few stalks of diced celery, diced garlic and diced red pepper, cooking until soft. Add a couple diced tomatoes (or use a 14 oz can), a dash of ginger, ground marijuana, allspice, thyme, cayenne pepper, garlic sea salt and Tabasco. Bring to rapid boil for a couple minutes, stirring often. Add a cup of rice, stir well and cover the pan, cooking for about 15-20 minutes until rice is tender and has absorbed most of the liquid. During the last ten minutes of cook time, add in two pounds of de-veined and peeled shrimp (or crawfish), cooking until the shrimp curl. You can also cut back on the shrimp and add in some previously cooked ground sausage or simply add in a few strips of diced and cooked bacon for extra flavor. Sprinkle with green onion, ground marijuana and parsley; serve.

Shockingly Stuffed Sole

Preheat oven to 350. Melt four tablespoons of hash butter and add two tablespoons of flour, cooking for a few minutes over gentle heat until pale straw colored. Add a can of chicken broth and bring to a boil, then add in about an eighth of magic mushrooms, sliced, cooking until the sauce thickens. Add four tablespoons of heavy cream. Bring to a boil, then remove from heat, adding a splash of brandy, along with a half pound of cooked seafood (like shrimp, crab or crawdads; can be a combination of all three), a dash of Cajun seasoning, a dash of ground marijuana and an ounce of breadcrumbs. Skin the sole (or cod) and fill the side that was skinned with the mix (cut fillets in half along the natural line that divides them). Roll up, securing with a toothpick if necessary, and arrange in a baking dish greased with hemp butter. Spoon melted hash butter (about four tablespoons) over the top and cook for 20-30 minutes until fish is just firm.

Coco Crazy Cookies

Beat one cup of softened hash butter with a half cup of brown sugar, a half cup of granulated sugar, a large egg, a large egg white, a teaspoon and a half of vanilla, three quarter teaspoon of baking powder, a half teaspoon of salt and two and a half cups of flour. Add in three quarter cups of shredded coconut, a cup of white chocolate chips and a half cup of macadamia nut slivers. Drop in tablespoonfuls onto an ungreased cookie sheet, baking at 325 for 13 minutes or until lightly golden around edges.

Oat My Gosh Cookies

Beat one cup of softened hash butter with a half cup of brown sugar, a half cup of granulated sugar, a large egg, a large egg white, a teaspoon and a half of vanilla, three quarter teaspoon of baking powder, a half teaspoon of salt and two and a half cups of flour. Add in three quarter cups of quick oats, a cup of chocolate ships and a half cup of raisins. Drop by tablespoonfuls onto cookie sheet and bake at 350 for about ten minutes, until slightly golden around edges.

Cheery Cherry Cookies

Beat one cup of softened hash butter with a half cup of brown sugar, a half cup of granulated sugar, a large egg, a large egg white, a teaspoon and a half of vanilla, three quarter teaspoon of baking powder, a half teaspoon of salt and two and a half cups of flour. Add in a half cup of dried cherries, a quarter cup of crushed pecans, a half cup of white chocolate chips and a half cup of dark chocolate chips. Bake at 350 for about 11 minutes or until golden brown.

Cran Me Full of Cookies

Beat one cup of softened hash butter with a half cup of brown sugar, a half cup of granulated sugar, a large egg, a large egg white, a teaspoon and a half of vanilla, three quarter teaspoon of baking powder, a half teaspoon of salt and two and a half cups of flour. Add a half cup of quick oats, a half cup of dried cranberries, a half cup of white chocolate chips and a quarter cup of crushed walnuts. Drop by tablespoonfuls onto cookie sheet. Bake at 350 for 12 minutes until golden around edges.

Coco-Lemon Craze Cookies

Beat one cup of softened hash butter with a half cup of brown sugar, a half cup of granulated sugar, a large egg, a large egg white, a teaspoon and a half of vanilla, three quarter teaspoon of baking powder, a half teaspoon of salt and two and a half cups of flour. Mix in a half cup of chopped and toasted pecans, three quarter cups of shredded coconut flakes and a teaspoon of finely grated lemon peel. Roll dough into a log, coat the log with coconut flakes, wrap it in wax paper, freeze for an hour and slice cookies to be put onto an ungreased cookie sheet. Bake at 350 for about ten minutes, until edges golden. When they are done, glaze with a mix of a half cup of confectioners' sugar, two tablespoons of water and two tablespoons of lemon juice.

Zone Out Truffles

Bring one third cup of heavy whipping cream to a boil with six tablespoons of hash butter in a saucepan. Add two cups of double chocolate chips, a generous pinch of ground magic mushrooms and a generous pinch of ground marijuana, stirring until completely smooth and melted. Remove from heat and pour into a mixing bowl. Refrigerate two hours. Roll mix into one inch balls, and roll each ball in a combination of chopped almonds, a pinch of ground marijuana and coconut flakes.

Sweet Daze Treat

Cook 8 oz of lasagna noodles according to package; drain and set aside. In a large bowl, beat four eggs with a half cup of sugar, a cup of cottage cheese (small curd), a cup of sour cream, a cup of milk, a quarter cup of ground marijuana, a cup of chocolate chips, a cup of coconut flakes, a half cup of Kahlua and one third cup of melted hash butter. Layer this mix with noodles in a baking dish greased with hash butter, leaving a noodle layer on top. In a small bowl, combine a half cup of flour, a quarter cup of brown sugar, a generous sprinkle of ground marijuana, a half cup of chocolate chips and a teaspoon of instant chai tea mix. Using fingers, rub a quarter cup of hash butter, chilled and cut into pieces, working it into the mix to form coarse crumbs. When ready to bake, sprinkle topping evenly over the noodle layers. Bake at 350 until firm in center, about an hour. Cool, cut into squares and serve topped with a fresh marijuana leave and whipped cream.

Totally Baked Cheesecake

Prepare a crust using three quarter cups of finely crushed Oreo cookie crumbs, a half cup of graham cracker crumbs, a quarter cup of melted hash butter, a quarter cup of dried cherries, two tablespoons of sugar and a generous pinch of ground marijuana, mixing the ingredients and pressing them into the bottom and sides of a pie tin. In a large mixing bowl, blend a pound of softened cream cheese, three eggs, a cup of sugar, a quarter cup of heavy whipping cream, a quarter cup of Kahlua, a cup of white chocolate chips, a half cup of coconut flakes, a teaspoon of vanilla and a quarter cup of ground marijuana. Pour this mix into the pie and bake at 350 for 45 minutes. Top with a mixture of a cup of whipped cream, a quarter cup of coconut flakes, a quarter cup of cherries, a generous pinch of ground marijuana and a quarter cup of white chocolate chips. Serve with an Oreo cookie on each slice.

Butterscotch Lose Track of Watch Cookies

Beat one cup of softened hash butter with a half cup of brown sugar, a half cup of granulated sugar, a large egg, a large egg white, a teaspoon and a half of vanilla, three quarter teaspoon of baking powder, a half teaspoon of salt and two and a half cups of flour. Add in a half cup of butterscotch chips, a half cup of toffee pieces, a half cup of oatmeal and a half cup of chocolate chips. Drop by the teaspoonful onto cookie sheet and bake at 350 for about ten minutes.

Butter Than Smoking Stew

In a large pot, cook a pound of diced boneless skinless chicken with a minced garlic clove, three tablespoons of hash butter, a diced onion, a diced sweet pepper, a few diced celery stalks, a half cup of sliced magic mushrooms, and a couple handfuls of fresh marijuana leaves. As chicken is cooked, add in a can of diced tomatoes with chilies or jalapenos, two cans of chicken broth, two cans of water, two cans of butter beans, about 8 oz of alphabet noodles, a small can of corn, a pinch of Italian seasoning, a generous pinch of ground marijuana, a pinch of Cajun seasoning and a pinch of turmeric.

Sticky Icky Buns

Mix a box small box of butterscotch pudding, not instant, with a cup of nuts, a cup and half of hemp butter and a cup of brown sugar. Stack a package of 36 frozen rolls in two Bundt pans well greased down with magic mushroom butter. You can also use an angel food cake pan or put them into round baking dishes for the pull-apart kinds of buns. Pour the hemp butter mix over that. Cover with foil and a towel and let stand over night at room temperature. Bake for 30 minutes at 350 and allow to cool ten to twelve minutes before removing from the pan.

Mango's Crazy Cake

Preheat oven to 350 and grease a 13 x 9 pan with hemp butter. In a large bowl, combine two cups of flour, two cups of sugar a teaspoon and a half of baking powder, a half teaspoon of baking soda, a half teaspoon of ground nutmeg, a quarter teaspoon of salt and a tablespoon of ground marijuana. Cut in a half cup of hash butter until mixture resembles crumbs. In a small bowl, combine a cup of buttermilk with two beaten eggs and a teaspoon of vanilla. Mix this into the flour mix. Fold in three cups of coarsely chopped de-seeded and peeled mango (about three). Spread into prepared pan. Combine one third cup of sugar with three quarter teaspoons of cinnamon and sprinkle over batter. Bake 40 minutes or until a wooden toothpick comes out clean from center. Cool slightly but serve warm with whipped cream. Instead of using buttermilk, you can also make sour milk by adding a tablespoon of lemon juice to a cup of milk and allowing it to stand for a few minutes.

Low Key Gnocchi

In a large sauce pot boil six large russet potatoes, peeled and sliced, until fork tender. Drain. Mash potatoes. In a small bowl, combine two beaten eggs, a teaspoon of garlic sea salt, a teaspoon of white pepper and a tablespoon of ground marijuana. On a smooth surface form the potatoes into a well and pour the egg mix into the well. Work the mix gradually with both hands, gradually adding three cups of flour, scraping the dough up from the work surface when needed. Dust the dough with flour as long as it feels sticky, but try to keep the gnocchi light, using as little flour as necessary. Cut the dough into six equal parts. Roll each piece into a half inch thick rope, then slice it into half inch dumplings. Indent each dumpling with your thumb. Bring about six quarts of water to boil, lightly salting it. Cook gnocchi a few at a time, stirring gently and continuously with a wooden spoon until they rise to the surface, a couple minutes. Remove with a slotted spoon and transfer to a warm platter. To make sauce, in a large skillet over low heat, stir in a cup of hash butter, a diced garlic clove, a diced onion, a diced sweet pepper, a tablespoon of ground marijuana, a few cut up magic mushrooms and a dozen fresh sage leaves. Add a cup of heavy cream and cooked gnocchi (in batches if necessary), turning gnocchi gently until lightly coated and heated, a minute or two. With a slotted spoon, transfer gnocchi to a serving platter and sprinkle with parmesan cheese, pepper and shavings of ricotta. Serve immediately.

Hazy Hazelnut Frosting

In a small saucepan heat three tablespoons of heavy cream until it just bubbles around edges. Remove from heat and add a cup of chocolate chips. Let stand for a minute. Stir until chocolate is smooth. Meanwhile, in a large bowl, beat together a quarter cup of hash butter, room temperature, four tablespoons of Frangelico and a quarter teaspoon of salt. Beat in chocolate until fluffy, about five minutes.

Buzz Biscuits

Preheat oven to 400. Line a baking sheet with wax paper. In a bowl, combine one and a quarter cups of baking mix, a quarter cup of ground marijuana and a half cup of shredded cheddar cheese. Add one third cup of water and stir until just combined. Drop the dough by tablespoonfuls onto prepared baking sheet. Bake for ten minutes until firm and beginning to brown. While the biscuits are baking, melt a quarter cup of hash butter with a pinch of salt and a bit of chopped parsley. When biscuits are done, brush with hash butter sauce and serve.

www.ingramcontent.com/pod-product-compliance
Lightning Source LLC
Chambersburg PA
CBHW022029090426
42739CB00006BA/344